ON THE LOOSE WITH DR. SEUSS

Using the Works of Theodor Geisel To Develop
Reading, Writing & Thinking Skills

by Shirley Cook

Incentive Publications, Inc.
Nashville, Tennessee

Illustrated by Marta Drayton
Cover by Becky Rüegger
Edited by Leslie Britt

ISBN 0-86530-233-2

TABLE OF CONTENTS

PREFACE

Theodor Geisel was a man with a mission. He wanted to make reading fun for children because he felt that reading is the most important skill a child needs to develop to be successful in life. He thought that the best method to accomplish this is to amuse the audience while sneaking in some good old-fashioned learning along the way. Geisel, known to millions of fans throughout the world as Dr. Seuss, added one part mischief, one part love, one part lesson, and one part pure whimsy to create literature loved by children and adults alike. He wrote books for over fifty years, until his death in 1991 at the age of 87.

On the Loose with Dr. Seuss is a celebration of the works of Dr. Seuss and of the children young and old who continue to stand in awe of his genius. It is designed to acquaint students with Theodor Geisel, the person, and to promote a better understanding of the creative thought processes involved in the writing of Dr. Seuss's books.

Twenty-seven of Dr. Seuss's best-loved stories are used as springboards for discussions and activities in the areas of higher-level thinking skills, writing, and creative extensions. Teachers should have all students first read the assigned Dr. Seuss selection and then hold a class discussion on the book's subject matter, possible themes, characters, and moral implications. The exercises and activities in this manual are divided into four sections. First, background information on Dr. Seuss's life is provided. Quotes from Dr. Seuss, information on his family, and details on the specific books are presented for students in an accessible format. "Just Think!" exposes students to springboard research activities. "Let's Write" asks students to try their hands at a variety of research and creative writing activities. The section entitled "Imagine That!" combines creative thinking activities with art projects.

This book is designed to spark an interest in the entire reading and writing process for children of all ages. The pages may be duplicated for individual students, small flexible groups, or for whole group instruction.

DID I EVER TELL YOU HOW LUCKY YOU ARE?

BACKGROUND INFORMATION

Two weeks before his death, Theodor Seuss Geisel (Guy-zel) was asked by the *San Diego Tribune* if he had a final message for his public. He did and explained that whenever things in his life weren't going well he would tell himself, "You can do better than this." Dr. Seuss continued, "The best slogan I can think of to leave with the U.S.A. would be: 'We can do, and we've got to do, better than this.'"

In *Did I Ever Tell You How Lucky You Are?*, Dr. Seuss seems to discuss this same theme. He feels that human beings have a great deal of wonderful traits; however, he suggests that humans can certainly work to improve their lives in many ways. We could accomplish great things if we would only realize what we are able to do!

JUST THINK!

In *Did I Ever Tell You How Lucky You Are?* poor Harry Haddow couldn't make a shadow because something was wrong with his Gizz. We know, however, that in real life your Gizz has nothing to do with making shadows. A shadow is made when light shines on an object but cannot get through it. If you stand outside on a sunny day, your body will make a shadow on the ground as it blocks the sun. The size of the shadow will depend on the position of the sun in the sky.

You can make a shadow puppet by placing your hand between a light and a wall. A filmstrip projector without a filmstrip in it makes a good light source. Turn on the projector while it is facing a blank wall. Put your hand in front of the light, and try your hand at creating an interesting imaginary character. When you are satisfied with your character, sketch it on paper and give it a name.

Write or discuss three important things about your new character.

DID I EVER TELL YOU HOW LUCKY YOU ARE?

LET'S WRITE

Imagine that you are a left sock that has been mistakenly left behind in the Kaverns of Krock. How will you get home? In the space below, write about the adventures that you have on your way home.

Name:

DID I EVER TELL YOU HOW LUCKY YOU ARE?

IMAGINE THAT!

Imagine how hard poor Ali Sard had to work every Sunday painting the flagpoles in Grooz. Decorate this flag and flagpole in such a way that other students will know that it belongs to your class. Use bright colors and include things in your design that will remind other students of your room.

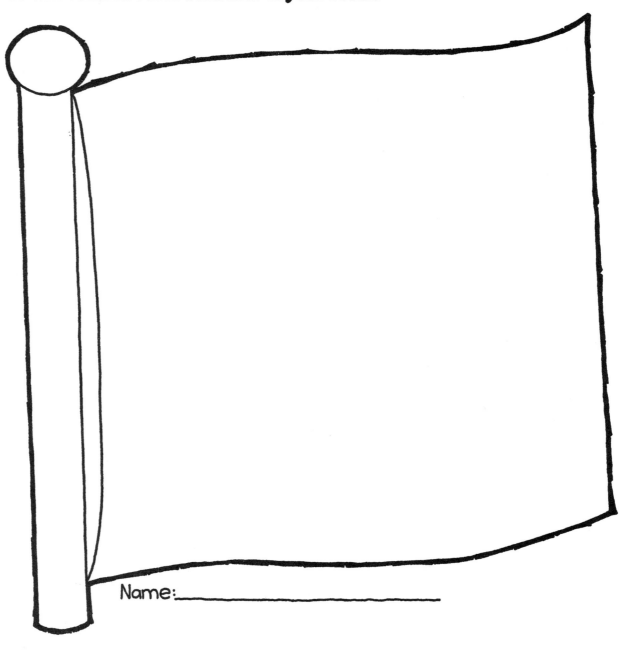

Name:_____

IF I RAN THE ZOO

BACKGROUND INFORMATION

Dr. Seuss often told people that his funny animals looked the way they did because he really couldn't draw. In fact, when he was in high school, his art teacher told him that he would **never** learn to draw. The teacher even suggested that Dr. Seuss skip his art class for the rest of the semester. Although he had no formal art training after high school, Dr. Seuss illustrated most of the books he wrote himself!

JUST THINK!

1. Gerald McGrew wished to change the zoo that he visited into something really special. The zoo was good enough as it was, but he found it just a little old-fashioned. Think of the last zoo that you saw. Compare that zoo to a zoo you would expect to find in the year 2050. How would they be different? Describe five ways that a zoo in the future might be different from a zoo of today. Draw one of the ways you feel it might be different.

2. Brainstorm with a friend to come up with a list of ten tiny animals and ten cute animals that could be found in a zoo today.

Great-Pronged Turtle

3. McGrew loved animals with horns. Of course, his horned animals were very unusual. List as many horned animals as you can think of that are living today. You may use reference books if necessary. When your list is complete, draw a picture of your favorite horned animal.

IF I RAN THE ZOO

LET'S WRITE

1. Although most zoos around the world house similar animals, you could create a zoo of really unusual animals if you went to a tropical rain forest to find your selections.

Research to find out some of the kinds of animals that can be found in a rain forest. Write five facts about one of these animals and draw a picture of it. If you were going to advertise it as a new zoo exhibit, how would you describe it? Write a paragraph that promotes your new zoo exhibit to the public.

2. McGrew would not stop until he had captured the world's biggest bird— the Fizza-ma-Wizza-ma-Dill—for his zoo. Research to find out the biggest bird actually alive in the world today. Answer these questions about it:

    a. Where is it found?

    b. How large does it grow to be?

    c. What types of food does it eat?

    d. How long does it usually live?

    e. What does it look like?

3. As McGrew explains, some beasts are too dangerous to catch with bare hands. Draw your idea for a machine that could be used to catch dangerous animals without harming them.

IF I RAN THE ZOO

IMAGINE THAT!

Create an entirely imaginary animal that you would like to have in your zoo. On a piece of white construction paper, draw a picture of your new creation. Be sure to color it brightly! Then, follow the steps below to create a cage for your new zoo animal.

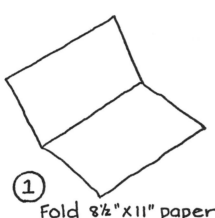

① Fold 8½"x11" paper (gray if possible).

② Mark 12 lines, each 1 cm. apart. Cut out every other pair.

③ Open paper and push cut section down in the opposite direction of the fold. Close the card with the cut section inside and press. Open, and the bars will pop up.

④ Fold a second 8½"x 11" piece of paper in half. Glue around the edges. Place the cage page on top and glue together. Now add your animal.

THE CAT IN THE HAT

BACKGROUND INFORMATION

In the 1950s, young children were reading from books known as the Dick-and-Jane books. Many educators did not approve of these books. Critic and author John Hersey wrote an article in *Life* magazine condemning these types of books as simple and meaningless. He issued a challenge to Dr. Seuss to write exciting supplementary reading books for children using a controlled vocabulary. Dr. Seuss took the challenge and received a contract and a public school word list from his publishing company, Random House.

Dr. Seuss thought that it would take almost no time to write a short book with easy words. He discovered that it was actually very hard work! What he thought would take two to three weeks took over a year of constant drawing, writing, rewriting, and changing. He became so frustrated at one point that he almost gave up. One day while looking through some sketches that he had thrown away, he found a sketch of a cat. He looked again at his word list and found the words "cat" and "hat." The cat in the stovepipe hat was born.

Dr. Seuss later became president of Beginner Books, now a division of Random House. He worked as president for many years and collaborated on other books with his wife and partner, Helen. He also used the pen name LeSieg to write other primary books. LeSieg is his last name, Geisel, spelled backward.

JUST THINK!

The activities that follow have been developed for younger children. The format has been simplified to take into consideration their need for space and controlled vocabulary.

THE CAT IN THE HAT

JUST THINK!

1. Sally and her brother were stuck inside on a rainy day. They could not think of anything to do. In the space below, list things that you could do if you were indoors on a rainy day.

Name:_____

On the back of your paper, draw your favorite thing to do on a rainy day.

THE CAT IN THE HAT

2. How would you answer the question posed at the end of *The Cat in the Hat*? Write your answer in the space provided below.

Name:_____

On the back of your paper, draw a picture of the Cat in the Hat in your bedroom.

THE CAT IN THE HAT

3. Find all of the hats that have words that sound like hat. Color them red.

Name: _____

THE CAT IN THE HAT

4. The fish in the story was very worried. He did not want the cat to be there when Mother was out. He did not like the mess that the cat was making. In the space below, make a list of rules to have at your house when you are playing alone or with friends.

Name:_____

On another page, draw your favorite indoors activity.

THE CAT IN THE HAT

LET'S WRITE

Dr. Seuss was handed a list of words by his publisher and asked to write a story for beginning readers. Write a beginner's book of your own using these words. You may, of course, add more words of your own choice.

bow	dish	run	house	play
now	wish	toy	no	hit
fish	fun	boy	go	bit

IMAGINE THAT!

If the Cat in the Hat came to your house while your mother was out, what kinds of things would he find to juggle? Draw or list them in the space below.

Name:_____

THIDWICK: THE BIG-HEARTED MOOSE

BACKGROUND INFORMATION

The story of *Thidwick: The Big-Hearted Moose* was created by accident. One day while Dr. Seuss was sitting at his typewriter trying to write, the telephone rang. It was his old friend Joe Warwick calling to ask if he and Dr. Seuss could get together for dinner the next night. During the course of their conversation, Dr. Seuss began to doodle. He talked and doodled for about twenty minutes. When he hung up, he realized that his scribbles looked a bit like a moose with other animals sitting on its horns.

So began the story of Warwick, titled in honor of his friend Joe. Dr. Seuss later changed the title to *Thidwick: The Big-Hearted Moose*. He would later joke by saying that if readers didn't like the story, it was not his fault. It was his friend Joe Warwick's fault!

JUST THINK!

1. Design a Guest Plaque in the space provided. On it, write the rules that you think are most important for guests to observe.

Name: _____

THIDWICK: THE BIG-HEARTED MOOSE

2. Do all horned animals shed their horns each year? Do some research to find out.

LET'S WRITE

Create a new animal guest who could arrive to live on Thidwick's horns. Draw it, and write a rhyming verse about it.

IMAGINE THAT!

When we say that a person is big-hearted, we feel that he or she has certain characteristics. What do you think some of these characteristics are? Write some big-hearted characteristics on the heart below. Circle the ones that you feel you have.

Which characteristic do you value most? Why?

YERTLE THE TURTLE

BACKGROUND INFORMATION

Theodor Seuss Geisel served in the United States Army during World War II as a member of the Army Signal Corps and Information and Educational Division. The films that he created for the army earned him the Legion of Merit.

It has been suggested that Dr. Seuss wrote *Yertle the Turtle,* the story of a greedy turtle king and his eventual fall from power, as a reaction against World War II fascism.

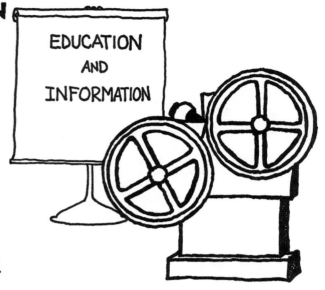

JUST THINK!

1. This story seems to tell us that it is important to stand up for what we believe despite what others say or do. Why is that sometimes hard?

2. What rules can we follow in order to be individuals rather than crowd-followers?

3. What gave Yertle the right to be king?

4. What do you think Dr. Seuss meant on the last page of the book when he wrote that all of the turtles and other creatures should be free?

YERTLE THE TURTLE

LET'S WRITE

1. Imagine that you are a newspaper reporter for a major newspaper. Your assignment is to go to the pond outside the Island of Sala-ma-Sond and interview ten of the turtles living there. (You may give the turtles any imaginary names that you desire.)

Write a news story describing how the turtles feel about King Yertle. Remember to include answers to the six reporter's questions: Who? What? Where? When? Why? How?

2. Mack, the small turtle on the bottom of the stack, is campaigning to become the new king. Help him write his campaign speech.

IMAGINE THAT!

1. Without looking at the pictures in the book, visualize the nine-turtle stack as your teacher or a friend reads the third page of the story.

Now, draw another type of animal stack with nine members. Color your drawing. Describe the ruler who would use it and how he or she would use it.

2. If turtles did not have shells, what do you think they would have instead? Draw one here.

©1994 by Incentive Publications, Inc., Nashville, TN.

GERTRUDE MCFUZZ
FROM YERTLE THE TURTLE AND OTHER STORIES

BACKGROUND INFORMATION

Theodor Seuss Geisel was born on March 2, 1904, in Springfield, Massachusetts. His father, Theodor Robert Geisel, was at one time a superintendent of the Springfield, Massachusetts, public park system. He has described his father as one of the world's great cynics. His father's cynicism may have been the result of the unfortunate circumstances in which he sometimes found himself. For example, Theodor Robert worked for twenty-five years at a brewery. On the day he was made company president, Prohibition was declared!

Henrietta Seuss Geisel, Theodor's mother, was a homemaker. Dr. Seuss used his mother's maiden name and his own middle name as a pen name for the majority of his literary career.

JUST THINK!

Gertrude McFuzz thought that more feathers would make her better than Lolla-Lee-Lou. They were a status symbol to her.

List five things that are status symbols for children and adults in our society today.

1. _____

2. _____

3. _____

4. _____

5. _____

Name _____

On a separate sheet of paper, discuss the importance to our quality of life of each status symbol.

GERTRUDE MCFUZZ

FROM YERTLE THE TURTLE AND OTHER STORIES

LET'S WRITE

Suppose that Gertrude McFuzz had been satisfied with three feathers. How would the story have changed?

Rewrite the story in your own words beginning with the line in which Gertrude McFuzz says she has three feathers and Miss Lolla only two.

Name:_____

(Use the back of the page if you need more room.)

GERTRUDE MCFUZZ
FROM YERTLE THE TURTLE AND OTHER STORIES

IMAGINE THAT!

With a partner, make a list of as many well-known children's songs as possible. Choose two favorites and practice singing the tunes as quietly as possible.

Once you feel comfortable with the tunes, begin writing your own lyrics for the songs. The lyrics should reflect your thoughts about jealousy and the idea that one person cannot be better than another.

Choose the one song that you feel is more successful, and perform your song live or tape record it for your class.

Example: Sing this song to the tune of "Old McDonald Had a Farm."

There are some people at this
 school—
 Oh yes, oh yes, there are—

Who think they're cool, and
 break the rules—
 Oh yes, oh yes, they are.

They mock your clothes and
 shoes and hair;

They're loud and rude, and just
 don't care.

I'm glad that I'm just me, it's
 true,

I like me, yes I do!

THE BIG BRAG
FROM YERTLE THE TURTLE AND OTHER STORIES

BACKGROUND INFORMATION

People have always wondered about the moral or message behind each Dr. Seuss book. Dr. Seuss has simply said that he tries to relate a message through the use of an analogy that both children and adults can grasp.

He has claimed that all storytellers are moralists whether or not they realize it because the children who read their stories are born with a strong ethical sense and will look for the moral in every story. Children want to see good rewarded and bad punished. The writer's job, according to Dr. Seuss, is to relate the message quietly but consistently without letting the audience see the message coming.

JUST THINK!

1. The rabbit and the bear held a bragging contest. List the kinds of things that people your age brag about.

a._____

b._____

c._____

d._____

e._____

Why do you think people brag?

_____

_____

_____

_____

_____

_____

_____

THE BIG BRAG

FROM YERTLE THE TURTLE AND OTHER STORIES

LET'S WRITE

1. Write a cure for bragging in the space below. Include the doctor's prescription, the advice to be given the patient, and the cost of the treatment.

PRESCRIPTION

Name:_____

2. Create a rhyme about bragging that will help braggers understand how their behavior makes other people feel.

Example:

When people start to brag,

I really want to gag.

The feats they are revealing,

They should be instead concealing.

At least, that's what I'm feeling!

I jumped this high!

THE BIG BRAG

FROM YERTLE THE TURTLE AND OTHER STORIES

IMAGINE THAT!

Compare the rabbit in this story to Peter Rabbit and the Hare from *The Tortoise and the Hare*. How are these three rabbits alike? How are they different? Write your response below.

Name:

HOW THE GRINCH STOLE CHRISTMAS!

BACKGROUND INFORMATION

Dr. Seuss created the character of the Grinch after pondering the meaning of the Christmas season for twelve months. However, it took

him only one week to actually write the book. Dr. Seuss explained later that he had been faced with a publisher's deadline and had never missed a deadline in his life. With only one week to go, Dr. Seuss began and finished his Scrooge-like story starring the Grinch. This impish character with the wonderful, awful ideas works hard to destroy the festive holiday spirit, only to discover that the Christmas spirit cannot be bought, sold, or stolen. Dr. Seuss, himself, claimed to be part Grinch. In fact, his license plates read G-R-I-N-C-H. *How the Grinch Stole Christmas!* was also made into a television special which won the Peabody Award.

JUST THINK!

How many words can you write that will rhyme with each of the following words from the story?

1. tight _____

2. heart _____

3. small _____

4. tree _____

LET'S WRITE

The Whos love to sing. Write a new song for the Whos to sing to the Grinch.

HOW THE GRINCH STOLE CHRISTMAS!

IMAGINE THAT!

Complete the Christmas Flip Puppet by following the directions listed below. When your puppet is finished, use it to tell to your friends and family the story of *How the Grinch Stole Christmas!*

1. Color and cut out the puppets on pages 32-35.

2. Write a summary of *How the Grinch Stole Christmas!* in four parts, and copy it onto the four puppets. Write what happens in the beginning of the story on Puppet 1 (page 32), what happens in the middle of the story on Puppet 2 and Puppet 3 (pages 33-34), and what happens in the ending of the story on Puppet 4 (page 35).

3. Glue or staple Puppets 1, 2, and 3 on top of Puppet 4 to make your Christmas Flip Puppet.

SCRAMBLED EGGS SUPER!

BACKGROUND INFORMATION

Dr. Seuss felt that one of the reasons for his success as an author of children's books was the amount of time and energy that he put into writing. He sometimes spent a year or two developing a single book. He would write and rewrite until the book was exactly as he wanted it to be. He felt that children could tell when a story had been put together without much thought, and he valued his audience too much to give less than his best.

Dr. Seuss once told a reporter that an adult audience might be easier to fool than a young audience, for if you lose the attention of a child for just one page, he said, your story will never be read.

JUST THINK!

Use a variety of reference books to answer the following questions.

1. What is the fastest bird that you can find? How fast can it travel?

_____

2. What is the name of the world's biggest bird? _____

_____

3. Which bird is the smallest bird?_____

4. Of all the birds you can find, which bird has the longest name?

_____

5. Which type of bird is endangered?

_____

6. Name an extinct bird.

_____

Name:_____

LET'S WRITE

Invent as many book titles with rhyming authors' names as you can.

EXAMPLES:
The Great and Magical Ice Cream Scooper
by Phineas Grouper

The Lakers Win Big
by Bartholomew Fig

Name: _____

IMAGINE THAT!

Dr. Seuss created a wonderful selection of imaginary birds who laid unusual eggs. The Kweet's eggs were sweet, while the egg of the Pelf was enormous.

Add your own imaginary bird to the collection. Draw it on the back of this page. What kinds of eggs would your bird lay? What would it eat? Tell about it in a rhyme.

DR. SEUSS'S SLEEP BOOK

BACKGROUND INFORMATION

Dr. Seuss's books have been translated into over twenty languages and are available throughout the world. One of the most unusual languages into which his books have been translated is Maori, the aboriginal tongue of New Zealand.

Dr. Seuss was most proud of having his books translated into Braille so they could be shared with the sight-impaired.

JUST THINK!

In *Dr. Seuss's Sleep Book*, Dr. Seuss describes the sleeping habits of some very unusual animals such as the Biffer-Baum Birds, the Hinkle-Horn Honking Club, and the Crandalls.

Find out about the sleeping habits of each of the following real animals. Describe where each of the animals sleeps and anything unusual about its sleeping process.

1. Hummingbird _____

_____

2. Bat (Any type)_____

_____

3. Black Bear _____

_____

4. Snake (Any type)_____

_____

5. Giraffe _____

_____

6. Fish (Any type) _____

_____

7. Butterfly_____

_____

Name:_____

LET'S WRITE

Using rhyme, describe the unique way that you and your family get ready for bed. Write your rhyme on a separate piece of paper.

Example:

Just outside of the town of St. Paul,
    the Cook family's having
    a pre-slumber ball.

They've turned on the stereo,
    cranked up the sound,
    and with p.j.'s and brushes
    are dancing around.

'Til each tooth is brushed,
    and each body gowned,
    and each little head
    on a pillow is downed.

Then they'll pause for a kiss,
    hear the chimes of
    the clock;
    then they'll pull up the
    covers and sleep like
    a rock!

©1994 by Incentive Publications, Inc., Nashville, TN.

IMAGINE THAT!

In *Dr. Seuss's Sleep Book,* the Offt weigh only minus one pound. In the space below, create an animal that would be even lighter than the Offt. Draw it, and describe it in detail.

Name:

THE 500 HATS OF BARTHOLOMEW CUBBINS

BACKGROUND INFORMATION

After graduating from Dartmouth College, Theodor Geisel began working toward a Ph.D. in English literature at Oxford University in England. However, he discovered that graduate work did not suit him, and he left Oxford to travel throughout Europe and draw. After writing his first children's book some years later *(And To Think That I Saw It on Mulberry Street)*, Geisel decided on the pseudonym Dr. Seuss. He added Dr. to his name to please his father, who had always wanted him to be a doctor.

In 1938 Dr. Seuss published his second children's story, *The 500 Hats of Bartholomew Cubbins*. The Children's Theatre Company in Minneapolis, Minnesota, is the only U.S. theater to have adapted a stage production of this book. It was performed in 1979, 1983, and 1988. Dr. Seuss apparently had liked the way the theater had presented a production of "The Little Match Girl," and so allowed them to adapt his book into a children's play.

JUST THINK!

Instead of a sword at his side, Sir Snipps, the hatmaker, wore a large pair of scissors. Instead of a sword at his side, Sir Alaric, Keeper of the King's Records, wore a long silver ruler.

List your name and the names of four other people you know well. If these five persons had lived during the time of Bartholomew Cubbins, what would each have worn at his or her side in place of a sword?

Explain your choice for each person.

LET'S WRITE

Write a sequel to *The 500 Hats of Bartholomew Cubbins* that describes Bartholomew's life as an adult. Be sure to explain how he uses the 500 gold pieces.

IMAGINE THAT!

If Bartholomew Cubbins lived during the twenty-first century, what would his last five hats look like? Draw and color them here.

Name:_____

It is reported that Dr. Seuss himself had a large collection of hats!

THE CAT IN THE HAT COMES BACK

BACKGROUND INFORMATION

As president of Beginner Books, a division of Random House Publishing, Dr. Seuss wanted children to delight in stories. He felt that children sometimes have trouble learning to read, and he wanted to make reading more fun for them.

The Cat in the Hat's success with parents and educators encouraged Dr. Seuss to revisit the mischievous cat. The sequel to *The Cat in the Hat* was written in 1958. *The Cat in the Hat Comes Back* was also quite successful and a wonderful supplement to early reading programs.

JUST THINK!

1. Find out about two different kinds of cats. Draw each one, and tell one fact about each.

Fact _____

Fact _____

THE CAT IN THE HAT COMES BACK

2. Draw a large X over each picture of something that The Cat in the Hat should not have done.

Color each picture of something The Cat in the Hat could have done to be helpful.

Eating cake in a tub

Shoveling snow

Putting spots on mother's dress

Going into the house without permission

Baking a pie

Leaving a ring in the tub

Drawing a picture

Cooking dinner

Using pop guns in the snow

Name: _____

THE CAT IN THE HAT COMES BACK

3. Draw a picture below of the funniest thing you think The Cat in the Hat did in the story *The Cat in the Hat Comes Back.*

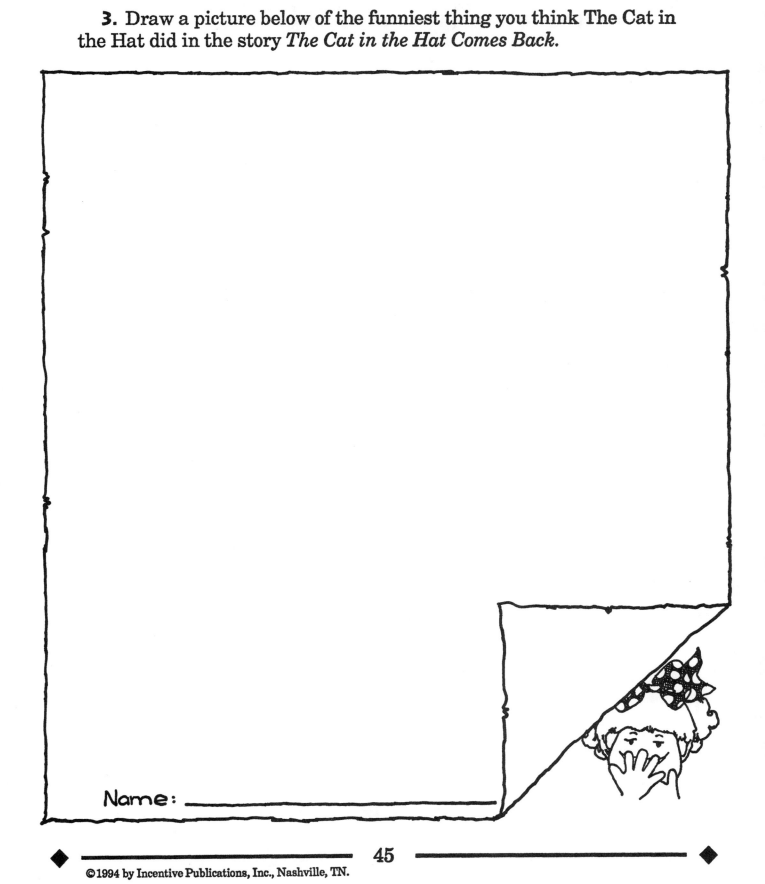

Name: _____

THE CAT IN THE HAT COMES BACK

LET'S WRITE: THE MINI-BOOK

cut out around the book

MY MINI-BOOK ABOUT

"THE CAT IN THE HAT COMES BACK"

NAME _____

MY FAVORITE CHARACTER WAS

_____

BECAUSE _____

_____

_____

_____

_____

THE FUNNIEST PART OF THE BOOK WAS _____

_____

_____

_____

_____

_____

THE HAPPIEST PART OF THE BOOK WAS _____

_____

_____

_____

_____

_____

DRAW THE SADDEST PART

DRAW YOUR FAVORITE PART

cut

cut

cut

THE CAT IN THE HAT COMES BACK

IMAGINE THAT!

Make a report card for the Cat in the Hat from *The Cat in the Hat Comes Back*.

Name:_____

_____School
Report Card

Grade: _____

Teacher: _____

A = Outstanding	D = Needs Improvement
B = Good	F = Unsatisfactory
C = Satisfactory	

Subject	Grade	Comments
Listens Well		
Follows Directions		
Works Well With Others		
Cleans Up After Himself		
Is Responsible		
Uses Thinking Skills		
Works Creatively		
Knows His Alphabet		

WACKY WEDNESDAY

BACKGROUND INFORMATION

Theodor Geisel assumed a variety of nicknames during the 1920s, the most famous of which was Dr. Seuss. Others such as Theo Seuss II and Dr. Theophrastus Seuss didn't stick for long. However, the one other pseudonym that Geisel continued to use on occasion was Theo LeSieg. LeSieg is simply Geisel spelled backward. When he used the LeSieg pseudonym, he often had someone else illustrate the story.

Such is the case with *Wacky Wednesday*. Although the author we lovingly know as Dr. Seuss wrote the book, it was illustrated by George Booth. Under the name LeSieg, Dr. Seuss published several Beginner Books for Random House Publishing. He was the president of the Beginner Book Division for many years, and all of these books display the famous "Cat in the Hat" on the cover.

JUST THINK!

Can you think of people you know who have done any of the following unusual things? Write your response on a separate piece of paper.

- A person who has worn socks of two different colors to school

  _____

- A person who has called the teacher "mom" or "dad" accidentally

  _____

- A person who likes to eat a very unusual type of food

  _____

- A person who can pat his or her head and rub his or her stomach at the same time

  _____

- A person who has thrown something valuable away

What *wacky* things have you done? List them on a separate sheet of paper, and discuss them with the rest of the class.

WACKY WEDNESDAY

LET'S WRITE

Write a W Story. What's that, you ask? Begin by brainstorming a list of words that begin with the letter "W." After your list is complete, make up a story that includes as many "W" words in it as possible. Remember to add something *wacky* to your story.

IMAGINE THAT!

Draw your own "Wacky Picture" below. Add 12 wacky events or items. See if a friend can find them when you are done.

Name:_____

HORTON HATCHES THE EGG

BACKGROUND INFORMATION

Dr. Seuss said that *Horton Hatches the Egg* was one of his favorite books. He called it the easiest to write and the one he had the most fun completing.

As was often the case, Dr. Seuss was simply doodling when in blew a sudden breeze. A picture of an elephant that he had drawn on tracing paper landed on top of a picture of a tree. Dr. Seuss looked at the new drawing and figured it would make a pretty funny story. He began writing the book in order to find out how that elephant actually got into the tree. Within a month, Dr. Seuss was in the middle of writing his story of an elephant playing mother to a bird.

JUST THINK!

Complete the discussion web below with three or four friends. Using your discussion as a base, list yes and no responses to the statement in the square. Be sure to tell why you feel the way you do.

YES　　　　　　　　　　　　　　　NO

An elephant is a better pet than a bird like Mayzie.

Name:_____

HORTON HATCHES THE EGG

LET'S WRITE

Find out what type of bird will hatch from each of the eggs below. Do some research on each bird, and write an interesting fact about it. Then draw each one below as it will look when fully grown.

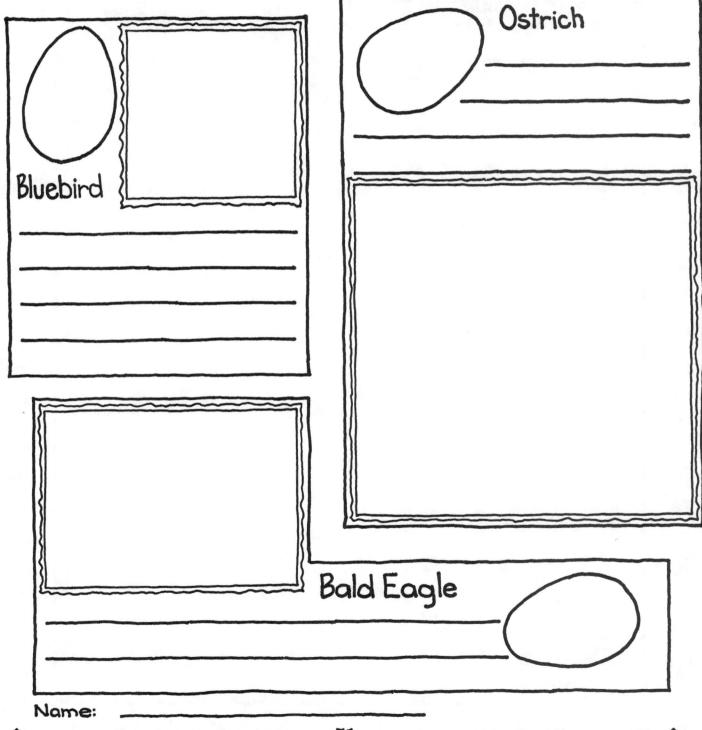

Bluebird

Ostrich

Bald Eagle

Name:

HORTON HATCHES THE EGG

IMAGINE THAT!

After Horton sat on the egg for nearly a year, the bird that hatched was more elephant than bird. Put two other animals together in a similar situation. Draw the animal that would finally hatch in the space below. Color it appropriately.

Name: _____

THE BUTTER BATTLE BOOK

BACKGROUND INFORMATION

The Butter Battle Book set a world record at the time of its publication by appearing on *The New York Times'* adult best-seller list for six months. It was written in 1984 and immediately became a hit with people from all walks of life. Politicians such as New York governor Mario Cuomo urged people to read the book in order to better understand the issues involved in nuclear war. By writing in simple, humor-filled language, Dr. Seuss defined a difficult problem quite clearly for children and adults alike.

At the time that *The Butter Battle Book* was written, Dr. Seuss was 80 years old. The book depicts an escalating arms race between the Zooks, who eat their bread with the butter side down, and the Yooks, who eat it with the butter side up. Each nation produces larger and more powerful weapons like the Big-Boy Boomeroo, and soon the leaders of each group confront one another with bombs in hand. Finally everyone is left wondering just who will drop the first bomb.

JUST THINK!

1. Humans have had disagreements over far more important issues than who butters their bread on what side. What are the most important issues that you feel countries have had disagreements about?

2. What issues, if any, do you feel are important enough to support by going to war?

3. Why would a nuclear war be so dangerous for the world?

4. Most of the time, wars are fought between two or more separate countries. Sometimes, though, a country has issues within its own borders that are as threatening as issues that create wars. What issues do we have in our own country that have caused people to dislike one another in an almost war-like way?

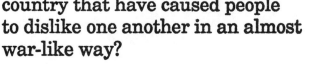

THE BUTTER BATTLE BOOK

LET'S WRITE

List the most significant aspects of two countries (do not include your own country) in the Venn diagram that follows. In the overlapping area, list ways in which the two places are alike. Then write a paragraph about the country you consider to be the stronger of the two, explaining why.

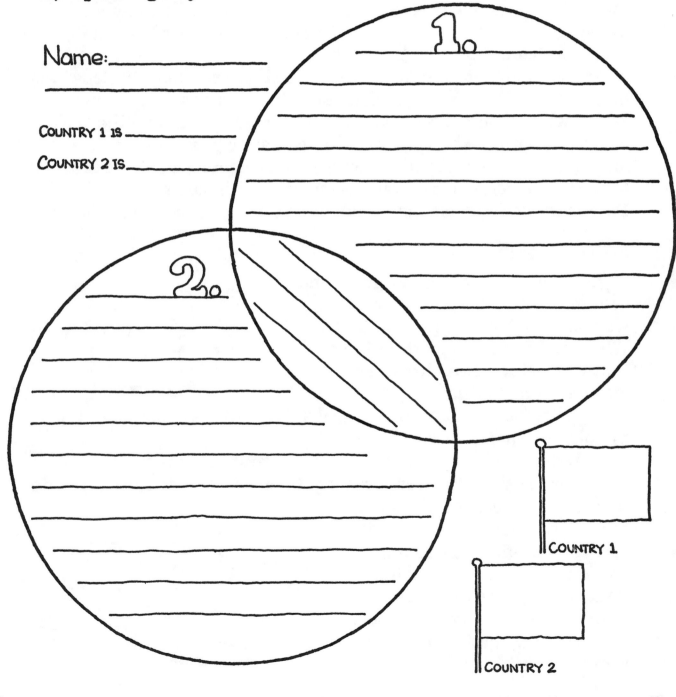

Name:_____

_____

COUNTRY 1 IS _____

COUNTRY 2 IS _____

1.

2.

COUNTRY 1

COUNTRY 2

THE BUTTER BATTLE BOOK

IMAGINE THAT!

Imagine that no one in the world had weapons of any type that could cause physical injury to another person. Create a new weapon that would attract someone's attention but wouldn't cause any harm. Draw it here and explain how it works.

Name: _____

OH, THE PLACES YOU'LL GO

BACKGROUND INFORMATION

This book was the last new book published for children by Dr. Seuss before his death on September 24, 1991. He was 87 years old at the time of his death and had written the book less than one year before. It was on *The New York Times'* best-seller list for over a year, breaking Dr. Seuss's own 6-month record held by *The Butter Battle Book.*

Oh, the Places You'll Go seems to best express the way Dr. Seuss approached life—with wonder, wit, and extraordinary exuberance. The book is almost a guarantee of personal fulfillment as long as we set our sights on the things we value and are willing to work hard for them.

JUST THINK!

1. We have all been to The Waiting Place at some time or another. We have all had to wait (and, perhaps, not always patiently) for something to happen. What are some tips that you can give to people in The Waiting Place when they become impatient? List them here:

a._____

b._____

c._____

d._____

e._____

2. Which of the tips is most helpful to you?

OH, THE PLACES YOU'LL GO

LET'S WRITE

If you could do or be anything at all, what would you do and what would you be? Write about the most perfect way that you can think of to spend your life.

IMAGINE THAT!

1. If you could trade places for one week with three people that you consider to be famous or important, who would they be? Why? What would you most want to do during each week?

2. Create a word-find puzzle of people that you consider to be heroes. Include at least twenty-five names in your puzzle.

3. List the three most important qualities that you think a person needs in order to be successful. Rank them in order of importance and explain why you chose each one.

1. _____
_____
_____
_____
2. _____
_____
_____
_____
3. _____
_____
_____
_____

Which of these qualities do you feel you have?

BACKGROUND INFORMATION

Dr. Seuss loved to read. In fact, he made it a practice to read four or five books each week. Dr. Seuss thought that one reason some children do not learn to read very well is that they spend too much time watching television and not enough time reading books. He felt that while children's television has many good things to offer, children do not always have good judgment about how much television to watch. Dr. Seuss wanted children to use some of the peak morning time for reading rather than for television-viewing. He urged parents to limit the amount and ensure the quality of their children's television time.

JUST THINK!

Answer the following questions on a separate sheet of paper:

1. Describe what you think makes one person feel he or she is better than, or more important than, another person.

2. List anything that you can think of that is absolutely 100 percent guaranteed.

3. What types of symbols do we use in the United States that show one person to be more important than, or better than, another person? (Example: a star on the door of a person's dressing room)

4. Before the United States of America declared independence, it was ruled by England's king. This type of government is called a monarchy. Describe the kind of class system that is established in a monarchy.

5. In groups of three, use the web below to brainstorm a list of attributes that you find appealing in other people. Brainstorm until you have written at least 15 attributes.

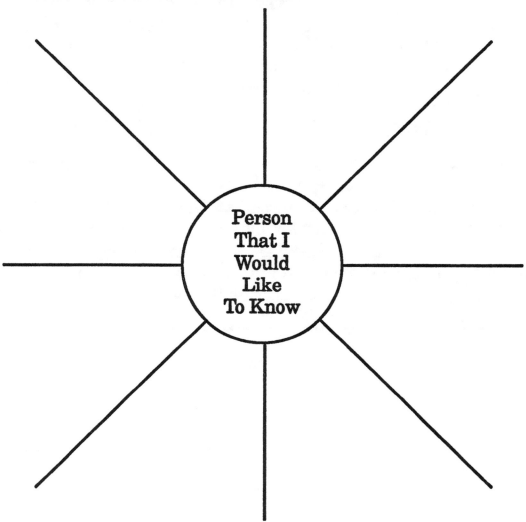

Person That I Would Like To Know

When your group has completed its web, rank in order of importance to you the attributes you have listed. Share your results with other groups. How do your top five attributes compare to those of other groups?

Name_____

THE SNEETCHES AND OTHER STORIES

LET'S WRITE

Sylvester McMonkey McBean guaranteed his work 100 percent. On a separate piece of paper, write a newspaper, magazine, or television ad for a product or service that you feel never fails—something that never lets the customer down.

IMAGINE THAT!

Throughout history, people have developed symbols that represent a level of superiority. In the story *The Sneetches*, the star was such a symbol. In Hollywood, the star is also a symbol indicating the best.

Invent a design that could be used as a symbol of equality. It should be a symbol that shows that all people are of equal value. Create your symbol below, and describe its significance.

THE ZAX, TOO MANY DAVES, AND WHAT WAS I SCARED OF?

(FROM THE SNEETCHES AND OTHER STORIES)

BACKGROUND INFORMATION

While Theodor Geisel was studying at Oxford University in England, he met Helen Palmer, another American student studying literature. Palmer encouraged him to pursue his interest in art. Partly because of Helen's encouragement, Geisel left the university to travel through Europe and draw. He developed humorous cartoons for such magazines as *Judge, Vanity Fair, Liberty,* and *Life* while he traveled.

When Geisel returned to the United States in 1927, he married his former classmate, Helen, who remained his wife and business partner for forty years until her death in 1967. They did not have any children.

JUST THINK!

1. It is sometimes said that history repeats itself. What does this phrase mean? How is it demonstrated in the stories found in *The Sneetches and Other Stories*?

2. Play a game of Guess the Character. Each player makes up a three-clue riddle that describes a character from one of Dr. Seuss's books. Divide into small groups, and read the riddles in turn. Everyone guesses who the character is as the clues are read.

Example:
   Clue 1: "I speak for the trees."
   Clue 2: "I tried to help the Brown Bar-Ba-Loots."
   Clue 3: "I was lifted away."
   "Who am I?"
(Answer: The Lorax)

THE ZAX, TOO MANY DAVES, AND WHAT WAS I SCARED OF?

(FROM THE SNEETCHES AND OTHER STORIES)

3. If there had been 23 children in your family and you could have helped to name each one of them, how would you have chosen to name them?

LET'S WRITE

Write a story to go with one of the following titles:

1. "The Star-Belly Sneetches Go Camping"

2. "A Day in the Life of the McCaves"

3. "The Zax, the Fax, and the Alto-Sax"

4. "Pale Green Pants Invade U.S. Cities"

5. "The Day I Met the Sneetches"

IMAGINE THAT!

A logo is a symbol that represents a word, person, or company.

This example represents a company known as The Literature Link.

Create a logo for two of Dr. Seuss's characters below. Then create a logo for yourself on a separate sheet of paper.

AND TO THINK THAT I SAW IT ON MULBERRY STREET

BACKGROUND INFORMATION

This is the first book that Theodor Geisel wrote for children, and he claimed that the idea for it was purely accidental. At the time, Geisel was employed as an advertising illustrator. He worked creating different characters to help advertise a variety of products. His most remembered advertising campaign was created for Standard Oil of New Jersey, for whom he developed insecticide ads. Later he liked to tell people that he had drawn bugs for seventeen years, and they all looked silly.

In 1936, while crossing the Atlantic by ship, he amused himself by coming up with words to go along with the rhythm of the ship's engine noises. These words became the text for *And To Think That I Saw It on Mulberry Street*. When he reached shore, he began to illustrate his story. After Dr. Seuss's story was complete, he presented it to at least twenty-nine publishers before it was finally accepted by Vanguard Press. Most of the publishers who turned down his work said that it was so unlike any other children's book, with its sing-song sort of verse, that it didn't have much chance of commercial success!

JUST THINK!

1. Try to remember as many things as you can that you saw on the way to school this morning. List them. When you come to school tomorrow morning, see how many things you missed on your list.

AND TO THINK THAT I SAW IT ON MULBERRY STREET

2. How observant are you? See how many of the following questions you can answer quickly, without checking the answers.

   a. What letters are found on the number 5 on the telephone dial?
   b. Does your bedroom door open into the room or into the hall?
   c. When you fold your hands, which thumb is on top?
   d. What color are your best friend's eyes?
   e. On a girl's blouse, are the buttons on the left side or the right side?
   f. On a traffic light, where is the green light located?
   g. How many sides does a stop sign have?
   h. What colors are on your state's license plates?
   i. Who appears on the ten dollar bill?
   j. Which sock do you put on first in the morning?

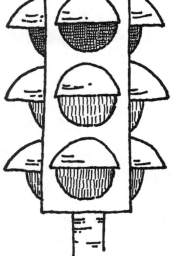

LET'S WRITE

Listen to a tape recording of instrumental music (music without words) for at least five minutes. Then listen to the same music again. This time, write down all of the words that you think of while listening to the music.

Turn the music off. Create an imaginary story using as many words from your list as possible.

AND TO THINK THAT I SAW IT ON MULBERRY STREET

IMAGINE THAT!

How would you change *And To Think That I Saw It on Mulberry Street* to update it to the late twentieth century? What would you want to see on the way down Mulberry Street? Illustrate and describe two of your ideas below.

TWENTIETH CENTURY··· HERE WE COME!

Name:

THE KING'S STILTS

BACKGROUND INFORMATION

Dr. Seuss is most famous for the humorous, off-beat poetic style that he developed early in his career; however, his third children's book, *The King's Stilts*, was written as a narrative. This was his first book to be published by Random House, with whom he remained associated for the rest of his life. *The King's Stilts* has been a children's favorite for over 50 years.

Dr. Seuss insisted that his writing be fun. He said that when he decided to leave Oxford, he also decided to remain a child for as long as he could. His wife and business partner, Helen (Palmer) Seuss, said simply that her husband wrote to amuse himself. Luckily, what amused Dr. Seuss has also amused boys and girls of all ages since the late 1930s. At the time of his death in 1991, his books had sold an estimated 200 million copies. It is an amazing feat that all of his children's books are still in print today!

JUST THINK!

Play a game of Vocabulary Memory. Begin by learning the meanings of the vocabulary words on the cards. In your mind, practice matching

the correct word to its correct meaning. With a partner, place the word and meaning cards face down in an area in front of you. Player 1 begins by choosing a card. He or she reads the card and shows it to Player 2. The card is then placed face up in the space from which it was taken. Player 1 then takes a second card. Again it is read to Player 2 and placed face up in its spot. If the two cards match, both cards are kept by the player making the correct match. If the word and meaning do not match, the cards must be placed face down once again. When a match is made, the player making the match receives another turn. The game continues until all cards have been matched. The player with the most matches is the winner.

VOCABULARY MEMORY

Teacher's Note: Use index cards to make two sets of cards: one for meanings and one for words.

Undignified	Not worthy of high esteem or honor
Stilts	Two poles, each with a rest to elevate the wearer and permit walking
Scowler	A person with a threatening look
Declared	Stated with authority and emphasis
Slanting	In a sloping direction
Hoarse	Rough-sounding
Nervous	Easily excited; jumpy
Stammer	A halting and/or repetitive pattern of speech
Impudent	Lacking respect for others
Groping	To search blindly
Pomp	A show of magnificence
Dignity	The quality of being honored or esteemed
Bellowed	Yelled

THE KING'S STILTS

LET'S WRITE

The Kingdom of Binn is unusual for several reasons. With a partner, create your own unique kingdom. Write about it in such a way that anyone reading about it will feel as though he or she has been there. Be sure to include information such as:

1. The way the kingdom looks
2. The location of the kingdom
3. Unusual animal life
4. Unusual plant life
5. How the people make a living
6. Information on the royal family
7. Description of the people of the kingdom

Draw a detailed sketch of one important part of the kingdom.

IMAGINE THAT!

You and your partner have been elected as town historians for your new kingdom. Your job is to compile a time capsule that will help people of future generations learn about the life of your kingdom's society.

Your time capsule will be an envelope. Using six small pieces of paper that will fit inside your envelope, draw and describe six important things found in your kingdom. These six drawings will represent your kingdom's artifacts.

When your artifacts have all been placed into your envelope, seal it. You may exchange your time capsule with another team.

After the exchange, pretend that you are living in the year 2100. You have just discovered a time capsule while on an archaeological dig. Open the capsule and carefully examine each artifact. Based on this historical evidence, write a story about the kingdom you have unearthed. Give as much information as you possibly can based on the artifacts. When you are finished, you can compare your story with the original story about the kingdom. Use the chart on page 69 to help you evaluate how well you and your partner made predictions.

THE KING'S STILTS

Facts You Predicted That Were Part of the Original Story:

Facts You Were Not Able to Predict:

Name:_____

Were there facts you did not predict that you should have known about based on the artifacts? Circle them.

THE LORAX

BACKGROUND INFORMATION

Dr. Seuss worked for two years on *The Lorax*, a book he often claimed was his favorite. When he began the book, he suffered from writer's block as he struggled to put together this tale of environmental pollution. Then he went to Africa. One day while watching a herd of elephants, he became inspired and wrote the book in less than two hours. Dr. Seuss said he couldn't explain it, but that sometimes a writer just has luck!

As people today struggle to protect the environment, the words of the Lorax seem to remind all of us that our work to keep our planet healthy is important indeed. The experiences of Truffula Trees, Brown Bar-ba-loots, Humming-Fish, and Swomee-Swans may be more real than we think, and the words of the Lifted Lorax contain a message that's truly more fact than fiction.

JUST THINK!

1. Create a list of products that you feel do not harm the environment.

2. Describe what you would do if you had been given the last Truffula seed.

3. Create a story map of *The Lorax* using the map organizer provided on page 71.

4. What types of environmental concerns do you have in the area of the country where you live? What are you doing to try to help solve the problems?

Story Map — THE LORAX

Setting
    Characters:_____
    Place: _____

⬇

Problem

⬇

Goal

⬇

Event 1

⬇

Event 2

⬇

Event 3

⬇

Event 4

⬇

Event 5

⬇

Event 6

⬇

Solution

Name_____

THE LORAX

LET'S WRITE

Now that you have finished reading *The Lorax*, write a letter to a person you know telling him or her why you think the book is important. Also, explain why you feel that everyone should know more about the environment.

Date _____

Dear _____ ,

I have just finished reading the book *The Lorax*. I thought this book was important because

I think you should know more about the environment because

Sincerely,

IMAGINE THAT!

Compare the trees of the rain forest to the Truffula Trees!

HORTON HEARS A WHO!

BACKGROUND INFORMATION

Dr. Seuss, like the rest of us, had his own favorites from among the characters he created. He once told an interviewer that he particularly liked Horton and would have been glad to have dinner with him. He also said that he wouldn't have been caught dead with some of his other characters.

Dr. Seuss created Horton in 1940 when he wrote his first Horton tale, *Horton Hatches the Egg*. In his sequel *Horton Hears a Who!*, the compassionate main character, Horton, finds himself risking his life to protect the rights of all people.

JUST THINK!

Create a "Who Am I?" Riddle on the form provided on page 74.

LET'S WRITE

1. Complete a book summary on the *Horton Hears a Who!* Book Report Pyramid (page 75).

2. Complete the *Horton Hears a Who!* Story Frame (page 76).

IMAGINE THAT!

Draw the way you imagine Horton's home, the "Jungle of Nool," looks.

WHO AM I?

Which Dr. Seuss character do you like best? Write a riddle about your favorite Dr. Seuss character for your school's newspaper. Write five clues (in complete sentences) about your character. Use a Dr. Seuss book to help you find interesting information for your riddle. Give your riddle to other classmates, and see if they can guess the character.

_____

_____

_____

_____

_____

_____

_____

_____

_____

_____

_____

Reporter _____

Book Report Pyramid: **HORTON HEARS A WHO!**

Name _____

(Begin at the bottom and work your way to the top.)

How

Why

What

When

Where

Who

Author

Name of Book

Story Frame: **HORTON HEARS A WHO!**

Name _____

Create a third Horton story with the help of this story frame.

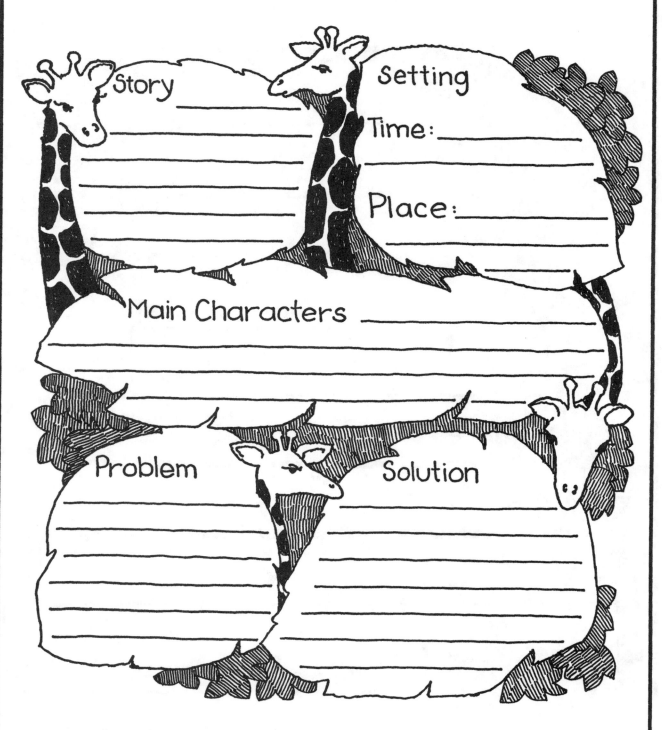

Story _____
_____
_____
_____
_____

Setting

Time: _____

Place: _____
_____

Main Characters _____
_____
_____

Problem _____
_____
_____
_____
_____
_____

Solution _____
_____
_____
_____
_____

Write the complete story after your teacher or partner has reviewed your story frame.

76

IF I RAN THE CIRCUS

BACKGROUND INFORMATION

Dr. Seuss enjoyed drawing funny zoo and circus animals. He once told a reporter that he would have preferred to have drawn beautiful ladies for a living but he never could figure out how to draw their knees correctly.

In *If I Ran the Circus*, Dr. Seuss uses his imaginative genius to create some of the Seussian animals that are loved by people all over the world.

JUST THINK!

Play a game of Homophone McGurkus (page 78).

LET'S WRITE

1. Morris McGurk described his circus as colossal, stupendous, astounding, fantastic, terrific, and tremendous. List other words that have a similar meaning.

1. _____	6. _____	11. _____
2. _____	7. _____	12. _____
3. _____	8. _____	13. _____
4. _____	9. _____	14. _____
5. _____	10. _____	15. _____

Describe a circus animal act by using five of the words you listed.

2. Complete the Circus Animal Observation worksheet (page 79) using an animal from your own imagination.

IMAGINE THAT!

Create your own special circus act for the circus parade. Add it to the classroom collection to make a room parade.

Teacher Directions: **HOMOPHONE McGURKUS**

Have the students play a game of Homophone McGurkus using the homophones listed below. The students work in pairs and secretly choose a pair of homophones. Each pair of students makes up a sentence using each of the words. In place of the homophones, however, they use the word "McGurkus." The sentences are then read aloud, and the class must guess which homophone pair was used. Both sentences should be read before anyone makes a guess.
(Example: My McGurkus got so tangled by the wind that I can't comb it. I don't believe that McGurkus didn't beat the turtle in the race. Homophones: hair; hare.)

You may wish to project the words on the overhead or display them on the board.

1. there — their
2. tale — tail
3. sea — see
4. two — to
5. would — wood
6. ate — eight
7. I — eye
8. hear — here
9. no — know
10. one — won
11. nose — knows
12. new — knew
13. red — read
14. piece — peace
15. where — wear
16. night — knight
17. our — hour
18. meat — meet
19. write — right
20. whole — hole
21. by — buy
22. mane — main
23. flour — flower
24. Jim — gym
25. pair — pear
26. for — four
27. be — bee
28. blue — blew
29. hair — hare
30. horse — hoarse
31. son — sun
32. road — rode

CIRCUS ANIMAL OBSERVATION

Kind of circus animal: _____

Animal's name: _____

Size of animal: _____

Type of act it performs: _____

_____

What it eats: _____

_____

Where it is found in the wild: _____

_____

How long it lives: _____

Where and when it sleeps: _____

Your name _____

79

GREEN EGGS AND HAM

BACKGROUND INFORMATION

Green Eggs and Ham was written as the result of a bet that Theodor Geisel made with his publisher, Bennett Cerf. Cerf bet Geisel that he could not write a book using no more than fifty different words.

Of course, Dr. Seuss accepted the challenge. Not only was he able to write a book using only fifty different words, but he made it a best seller, too!

JUST THINK!

1. Complete the Rhyming Names Activity Sheet (page 81).

2. Complete the Dessert Survey (page 82). Interview 20 to 25 students and adults to find out which of the desserts found on the survey they would prefer to eat. Complete the graph and report your findings to the class.

3. Brainstorm to create a list of foods that you would enjoy having for breakfast more than you would enjoy green eggs and ham.

LET'S WRITE

Try your hand at the Sentence Puzzle (page 83). Cut each sentence apart, and then put the sentences in the same order in which they occurred in the story.

IMAGINE THAT!

Draw a picture of the best place to eat green eggs and ham. Do not use any of the ideas given in the story.

RHYMING NAMES

Sam-I-Am has a name that rhymes. His first name has the same end sound as does his last name.

Make ten rhyming names by matching these two lists. Write the rhyming last name on the line next to the first name with which it rhymes.

1. Jim_____ Brott

2. Nikki_____ McMann

3. Shelly_____ Ronseth

4. Ann_____ Tricky

5. Jack_____ Dreeve

6. Scott_____ Feruke

7. Candy_____ McMack

8. Luke_____ Quim

9. Beth_____ Blandy

10. Steve_____ Fonzerelli

Name _____

DESSERT SURVEY

Name _____

Data *(Use a tally mark each time a selection is chosen.)*

Chocolate Cake: _____

Pumpkin Pie: _____

Brownies: _____

Ice Cream (Any Kind): _____

Strawberry Shortcake: _____

Other: _____

Dessert Survey Graph

| | 24 22 20 18 16 14 12 10 8 6 4 2 0 | chocolate cake | Pumpkin Pie | Brownies | Ice Cream | Strawberry Short-Cake | Other |

SENTENCE PUZZLE

1. Cut the sentences apart.
2. Put them in the correct order.
3. Glue them onto a plain sheet of paper.
4. Read your summary.

Sam-I-am asks if his friend would like them in a house.

Sam-I-am asks his friend if he would eat green eggs and ham in the rain.

Sam's friend thanks him.

Sam-I-am asks if his friend likes green eggs and ham.

Sam's friend tells him that he would not eat green eggs and ham in a car.

Sam's friend says that he would eat them in a boat and with a goat.

Sam's friend tries the green eggs and ham.

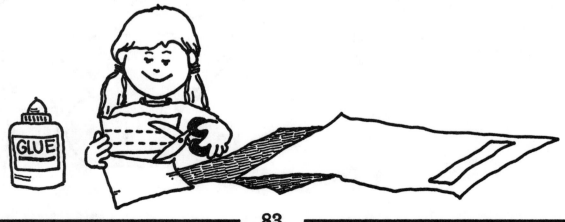

ON BEYOND ZEBRA!

BACKGROUND INFORMATION

Dr. Seuss's publisher, Bennett Cerf, thought highly of his celebrated author. Cerf said that during his time as a publisher at Random House he had worked with many talented authors—among them the great William Faulkner. He said, however, that he had only worked with one genius—Ted Geisel.

Dr. Seuss responded to Cerf's compliment in typical fashion, saying that he was no genius and had to work and sweat to put a book together. He said that even though his work may appear to have been completed in a matter of a few seconds, every single word was a struggle.

JUST THINK!

Dr. Seuss enjoyed inventing unusual animals and letters. What unusual animals or insects living today do you know about? Can you list one for each letter of the alphabet?

LET'S WRITE

Finish the Diary worksheet (page 85).

IMAGINE THAT!

Use your own creative genius to complete the One More Letter exercise sheet (page 86).

DIARY

If you were traveling with Conrad Cornelius O'Donald O'Dell, it would be wonderful to keep a diary. Pretend you are with Conrad and write about your visit to one of the letters. Use all of your senses (sight, smell, touch, taste, and hearing) to help explain your adventure.

January 1, 2100

Name: _____

ONE MORE LETTER

Name:_____

Go one step farther than *On Beyond Zebra!* Come up with your own new letter to add to the story. In the space above draw a picture of a word that you can spell with your new letter. Then fill in the information below.

My new letter looks like this: _____

A word that begins with my new letter is: _____

This word means: _____

MCELLIGOT'S POOL

BACKGROUND INFORMATION

Dr. Seuss dedicated *McElligot's Pool* to his father, Theodor Robert Geisel, in 1947. The year earlier Dr. Seuss had completed serving his time in the U.S. Army during World War II, and had also won his first Oscar for Best Documentary Short with his film *Hitler Lives*. Then, in addition to the publication of *McElligot's Pool* in 1947, Dr. Seuss and his wife, Helen, received a second Academy Award for *Design for Death*, considered the Best Documentary Feature of the year.

Dr. Seuss loved telling stories, and one of his favorites concerned his choice of a young Hollywood actor to play a part in a U.S. Army film entitled *Your Job in Germany*. His choices were Lt. Ronald Reagan and Sgt. John Beal. He chose Sgt. Beal. Little did he know that he was turning down a future president of the United States!

JUST THINK!

Conduct research about a fish of your choice. Record the information that you find on the Fish Family Album worksheet (page 88).

LET'S WRITE

Whip up a "Whale of a Story" on the story starter worksheet (page 89).

IMAGINE THAT!

Create a fish puppet from a paper bag. Be sure to color it brightly. If the fish were to swim into McElligot's Pool, what kind of conversation would it have with McElligot? Write a dialogue, and then act it out with your puppet.

FISH FAMILY ALBUM

by_____

Type of fish:_____

Size: _____

Weight:_____

Foods it eats: _____

_____

_____

Where it lives: _____

_____

_____

Baby Picture

How it defends itself: _____

_____

_____

Interesting facts: _____

_____

_____

_____

_____

Fin Print

A WHALE OF A STORY

Name:_____

BARTHOLOMEW AND THE OOBLECK

BACKGROUND INFORMATION

The idea for the story of *Bartholomew and the Oobleck* actually came to Theodor Geisel while he was serving in the U.S. Army. He was stationed in France where it rained day after day, night after night. Everyone became tired of being wet and cold all of the time.

One rainy night while walking through the mud and rain of a small French town, Geisel began to wonder if the rain would ever stop. Two American soldiers splashed by him, one muttering about the continual rain. Then the first soldier asked the second soldier why something new and different, something besides rain, couldn't come down.

As the two soldiers disappeared into the dark, Geisel thought that maybe something new could come down. He made a decision then and there to one day write about something new falling from the sky; however, he had to wait until the war was over. It would be several years later and 6,000 miles from his point of inspiration in France that Dr. Seuss would take pen in hand to create *Bartholomew and the Oobleck.*

JUST THINK!

1. Find out how fashion has changed since the days of the kings of the 1500s. Illustrate a time line extending from the year 1500 to the year 2000 of the changes in fashion for the royals or for the regular, everyday people.

2. Design an original puzzle on the It's A Puzzler worksheet (page 91).

IT'S A PUZZLER

Take a favorite part from *Bartholomew and the Oobleck*, and draw it on the puzzle below. Cut the pieces apart and share it with a friend.

Name _____

BARTHOLOMEW AND THE OOBLECK

LET'S WRITE

Choose nine sentences from *Bartholomew and the Oobleck* and copy down the first few words of each sentence in the spaces below. Have a partner work to complete the sentences.

1. _____

_____

2. _____

_____

3. _____

_____

4. _____

_____

5. _____

_____

6. _____

_____

7. _____

_____

8. _____

_____

9. _____

_____

Name_____

IMAGINE THAT!

Decide on something new that you would like to have come down from the sky. Then evaluate your decision with a PMI Inventory. "P" stands for the pluses of your decision. In what way would this new something be good or beneficial? "M" is for minuses. How would your new something be detrimental or bad? "I" simply stands for interesting. How would your creation be neither good or bad, but simply interesting? Based on this evaluation, have you created something that would be good or not so good for your town?

PLUSES	MINUSES	INTERESTING

Name: _____

BIBLIOGRAPHY

And To Think That I Saw It on Mulberry Street. New York: Vanguard Press, 1937.

Bartholomew and the Oobleck. New York: Random House, 1949 (Caldecott Honor Book).

The Butter Battle Book. New York: Random House, 1984.

The Cat in the Hat. New York: Random House Beginner Books, 1957.

The Cat in the Hat Comes Back. New York: Random House Beginner Books, 1958.

Did I Ever Tell You How Lucky You Are? New York: Random House, 1973.

Dr. Seuss's Sleep Book. New York: Random House, 1962.

The 500 Hats of Bartholomew Cubbins. New York: Vanguard Press, 1938.

Green Eggs and Ham. New York: Random House Beginner Books, 1960.

Horton Hatches the Egg. New York: Random House, 1940.

Horton Hears a Who! New York: Random House, 1954.

How the Grinch Stole Christmas! New York: Random House, 1957.

If I Ran the Circus. New York: Random House, 1956.

If I Ran the Zoo. New York: Random House, 1950 (Caldecott Honor Book).

The King's Stilts. New York: Random House, 1939.

The Lorax. New York: Random House, 1971.

McElligot's Pool. New York: Random House, 1947 (Caldecott Honor Book).

Oh, the Places You'll Go. New York: Random House, 1990.

On Beyond Zebra! New York: Random House, 1955.

Scrambled Eggs Super! New York: Random House, 1953.

The Sneetches and Other Stories. New York: Random House, 1961.

Thidwick: The Big-Hearted Moose. New York: Random House, 1948.

Yertle the Turtle and Other Stories. New York: Random House, 1958.

REFERENCE MATERIALS

Commire, Anne, editor. *Something About the Author.* Vol. 28 Detroit, MI: Gale Research Co., 1982, pp. 107-116.

Freeman, Don. "Dr. Seuss at 72—Going Like 60." *Saturday Evening Post* March 1977.

Kupferberg, Herbert. "A Seussian Celebration." *Parade* 26 February 1984.

Lamb, J.R. "Dr. Seuss Dies." *San Diego Tribune* 25 September 1991: A1, 8.

Morgan, Judith. "An Afternoon with Dr. Seuss." *Humpty Dumpty* (April–May 1992).

Moje, Elizabeth B. and Woan-Ru Shyu. "Oh, the Places You've Taken Us: RT's Tribute to Dr. Seuss." *The Reading Teacher.* Vol. 45, No. 9 (May 1992).